BABY LED WEANING

Guide

This book is a made easy baby led weaning guide that also serve as a cookbook with recipes your baby will cherish.

Cynthia

James

Table of Contents

About the Author

 Cynthia James is a world-wide expert in child development. Her love for children led her into the field and she hasn't looked back since. She has authored countless books on the different subjects ranging from children's health to family foods, and even the post-partum period. She is what you'll call a modern day scholar in child development.

She is married and blessed with three kids, Jasmine, Rachel, and Dylan. She is also a chorister and finds time to sing with the choir in her local church, and yes, she is blessed with a beautiful voice. Cynthia isn't your average mom as finds a way to balance her work, family and even squeeze out time for herself. She also frequents the gym and isn't afraid to stretch it out with a little yoga.

CHAPTER 1

BABY WEANING GUIDE

Let me start right off the bat and say that everybody loves babies. There's just something about them that brings a wave of joy, happiness and laughter to everyone's life. This is from the mother to the relatives, to the neighbors and to the public. They have a knack for turning things around and attracting a wave of positivity to steer things in the right direction.

When I had my first girl, Jasmine, I can remember that we weren't in the best place you'd want to be as a family, but we had to dig deep and turn the situation around to give her the best. In a way, she did bring out the best in me as a person and as a mother.

That aside, every parent wants the best for their child as they develop. What babies and young children eat and drink is critical to their physical wellbeing now and in the future. In that light, providing the best for your babies in terms of food and nutrition can be very tricky, especially for first-time mothers.

Navigating your way through the postpartum period can be challenging, especially when you don't have a lot of help. Well, all your calls just got answered as I'll be giving you the full lowdown on how to introduce solid foods to your babies. Just think of this as the ultimate guide to baby weaning.

Before we launch fully into the crux of the matter, let's get acquainted with the most important word about this subject: weaning. Weaning is a technical term used to describe the gradual introduction of solid feeds into the diet of infants and, at the same time, the withdrawal of the mother's milk supply. The World Health Organization (W.H.O) recommends that all babies be breastfed exclusively for the first six months, then progressively introduced to appropriate or solid foods after six months while breast-feeding for two years or longer.

Another keyword is a growth chart. It is critical to keep track of your baby's development. A growth chart is a simple yet accurate way to see if your baby is getting enough nutrients to grow. Always request that your baby's height and weight be recorded on a growth chart by your healthcare professional. Keep this chart in a safe place and bring it with you to the clinic or healthcare provider whenever you need to go for routine visits or if your baby is ill.

The process is different from culture to culture and is frequently governed by the child's individual needs. Healthy babies of weaning age grow and develop quickly, so it is critical to monitor them closely and ensure that they get enough of the right kind of food.

Weaning causes infants to start moving more and become much more independent of their mothers. They begin to have more contact with germs in the environment. So, despite the main aim of weaning your baby, ensure that you baby-proof their immediate environment so they don't come down with an illness.

As soon as the infant is no longer fed breast milk, he is considered fully weaned. So the purpose of writing this book is to assist all parents in starting their child's healthy eating habits off on the right foot. By the time your child is a year old, they should be able to eat the majority of the meals enjoyed by the remainder of the family.

Weaning can be a very unpredictable time for infants. Babies of weaning age do not grow well in many places. They frequently become ill and contract more infections, particularly diarrhea, than any other year. Undernourished babies may become even worse during the weaning period, and a baby may become malnourished for the first time during the weaning period. Many children of weaning age are stunted in their growth due to poor feeding and illness.

So take it upon yourself as parents and guardians to make sure that your babies are in a perfect health condition during the weaning process, as going through any change can be challenging, and you don't want to add health problems to their task.

Chapter 2

What Should You Be Expecting?

This is a crucial question to ask before going about the whole process. You don't want to dive right into the deep without knowing what to expect. Weaning your newborn child can be both exciting and terrifying; I can testify to that. Starting to eat solid foods is a big deal for your youngster. They've only had the tastes of milk and medicine up to this point. Now, there is a completely new world of flavors and textures to discover.

Breast milk is the first natural food available to babies. They are gradually weaned off it and introduced to the family's regular foods. To ensure that the entire process is successful, it must be closely monitored to make sure that the baby grows well and remains healthy.

Though some people claim that this is debatable, children are not born knowing how to eat, so don't be shocked if your child isn't sure what to do or if food is spat out in the first place. I can remember when this happened for the first time, I was pissed and happy at the same time.

As with drinking milk, some babies find weaning easier than others do. This further buttresses the point that no two individuals are the same, so avoid comparing your child to other babies or siblings. Every baby is unique, and it is up to you as a parent to find out what works for your kids and what pace they should follow.

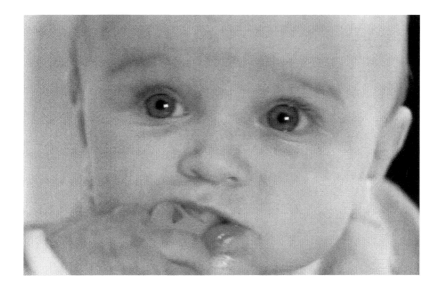

As I stated earlier, every baby is unique, so the parent has to observe and monitor their kids to know when they start showing signs of weaning. Yes, there are signs, and the ability to spot these signs will give you a head start, of the overall process.

Some general signs of readiness include:

1. Your baby can hold its head up and has excellent authority and neck control.

2. Your baby sits with assistance,

3. You'll notice that your baby's mouth closes around the spoon, and food remains in their mouths.

4. Children copy what they see other people do, and they can be very intuitive at this stage. You'll notice that your baby observes you as you eat and tries to find food for himself.

5. Do you know that period in which babies have a knack for putting everything into their mouth?

This is a very popular sign. You'll observe that your baby leans forward, and when they move forward, they open their mouth as food approaches.

6. Your baby can use his eyes, fingers, and mouth to look at the food, pick it up, and bring it to his mouth.

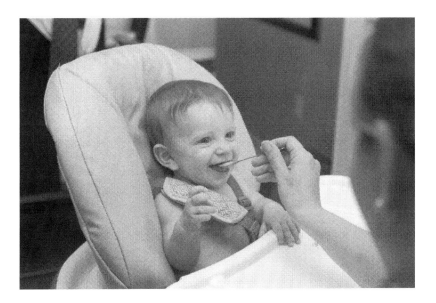

With weaning being a gradual process, there are classes of foods to introduce to your kid as the cycle goes on. They are essentially texture stages, and they are as follows.

Stage 1: Smooth semi-liquids are mainly prepared with a blender and could be one of three

1. Thin puree which runs quickly off a spoon or

2. Thick puree which can be eaten with a spoon

3. Regular puree, which quickly drops off a spoon.

Stage 2: They can be a fed thicker puree with tiny, very fine particles or lumps.

Stage 3: Here, mashed foods are typically blended. Thick puree with less sauce and a small amount of moisture is encouraged.

Stage 4: At this stage, soft chopped foods that have been mashed down with a fork should be given. The food should be thick, with little moist and soft lumps.

This gradual development overtime is usually divided into three weaning stages.

Stage 1 - Solid food introduction begins around six months.

Stage 2 - More textures and tastes begins around the age of seven months.

From 9 to 12 months, move on to **Stage 3**: the baby eats a wider variety of foods and family meals.

Though the periods listed above are general and gotten from research over time, it is important to know that some children may progress through the stages more quickly than others may. The essential thing is to introduce new textures to your child when they are ready. Now let us look at the stages individually.

STAGE 1 WEANING

The first stage of weaning is about 'first tastes' and experimenting with different foods, flavors and textures. This stage usually begins around six months and lasts for about a month, though some babies may start earlier.

HOW TO BEGIN WEANING

Your baby will only consume small amounts of food at this stage, perhaps one or two teaspoons. You should not expect a significant decrease in their milk (breast/formula) consumption.

6 MONTHS OF WEANING

Some babies may show signs of readiness to begin weaning before the age of six months. However, the World Health Organization advises waiting until your child reaches this age before starting solids. The main reason for this is that your baby's digestive system requires time to develop.

However, all babies develop at different rates, and some show weaning readiness as early as four months. If your baby was born prematurely (before 37 weeks), you should start introducing foods other than milk between the ages of 4 and 6 months. If you believe your child is ready to begin weaning before six months, I strongly recommend consulting a healthcare professional before deciding what to do next.

WHAT SHOULD BABIES EAT DURING THE FIRST STAGE OF WEANING?

Soft cooked vegetables such as carrots, pureed peas, and butternut squash are ideal to begin with. Make an effort to include as much variety as possible. You can also provide cooked or soft fruits as well as starchy foods.

WEANING IN THE SECOND STAGE

It is critical to begin introducing iron-rich foods around the age of 7 months. Babies born at full term and of a healthy weight have enough iron to last about six months. You don't want to run the risk of your child coming down with iron deficiency anemia. As a general guideline, begin Stage 2 after approximately 3-4 weeks of offering tastes and gradually increase from one meal per day to three.

The goal is to make your baby's food more interesting in terms of texture. It has been shown that introducing a wide variety of foods at this stage increases the kinds of foods accepted by a baby as they grow. You should start introducing finger foods to your baby as soon as they are seven months old.

WHAT FOODS CAN HELP WITH STAGE 2 WEANING?

At this stage, try to give your baby soft finger foods so that they have plenty of practice chewing foods. Iron-rich foods include animal protein (beef, lamb, or pork), dark poultry meat (chicken legs and thighs), and oily fish. Eggs, beans, lentils, chickpeas and hummus, fortified breakfast cereals, groundnuts or nut butter, and green, leafy vegetables are all vegetarian sources of iron.

Vegetarian iron sources are not as well absorbed as meat iron, but vitamin C in fruits and vegetables helps the body absorb iron from vegetable foods. As a tip, slowly cook the meats until they are very soft. You may need to mash some of the smaller ones as well.

WEANING IN THE THIRD STAGE

The third stage usually begins around 9 or 10 months of age, but it can occur later. Remember, each baby is different. During Stage 3, you will broaden the range of foods and textures available to your baby.

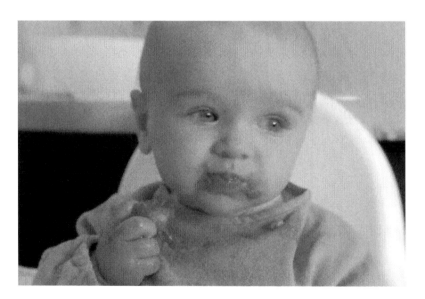

WHAT FOODS CAN HELP WITH STAGE 3 WEANING?

You can begin to introduce slightly tougher and crunchier finger foods to your baby at this point, such as raw vegetables and breadsticks. Try to include as many vegetables and other savory tastes as possible so that your baby is exposed to a variety of flavors and textures.

One of the most worrying things for parents during weaning is gagging. The sound of a baby gagging can easily be confused for choking. When food is introduced to a baby, it is normal for them to gag. The most important point to remember is that this is all new to your baby; some babies take longer to adjust than others.

Gagging is a normal part of the weaning process, and it is especially noticeable when transitioning from purees to lumps. After all, your child is learning how to handle new foods.

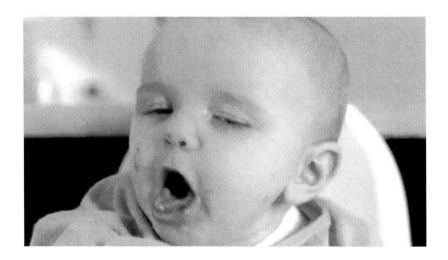

To reduce the risk of choking, keep any lumps and chunks small and keep an eye on your child while they are eating.

It is critical to introduce lumpy foods to help them develop their ability to:

1. speak

2. chew a broader range of foods, and

3. Broaden their dietary options, as they get older.

If you are having difficulty introducing food to your child or if they are refusing to eat at all, contact a health practitioner. It can be difficult when you're trying to introduce solid food to your baby, and it is rejected. Sometimes, it could affect you mentally, so never be silent when something like this happens and speak up, as professionals are always there to help.

As a rule, always stick to the following regulations when making food for your babies during this period.

1. Moisten their food with breast milk, formula milk, or water to the desired consistency.

2. Do not season your baby's food with salt or sugar. Remove their portion before adding salt to a family meal.

3. When preparing family meals for your child, avoid using stock cubes, gravy, packets, or jars of sauce.

Now, let's quickly address something that has been a matter of discourse over the past couple of years.

WHICH IS THE BEST: TRADITIONAL OR BABY-LED WEANING?

There are several approaches to weaning that you can take. These are frequently divided into two systems:

The first is called **traditional weaning.** This is the method in which parents frequently feed the baby with a spoon or hands.

The second is baby-led weaning. It is a method of weaning in which parents allow children to feed themselves.

Baby-led weaning is the more modern approach that can help your child develop independence while also fostering a positive relationship with food. However, in the long run, both methods achieve the same result.

Remember, weaning is a gradual process and not a complete and abrupt change in the feeding regime of an infant. Taking that into consideration, here are some tips on the best ways to combine milk feeds with weaning.

1. To keep your baby from becoming unduly hungry, try giving half a milk feed before introducing solids. After that, you can provide the rest of the feed.

2. Incorporating these milk feeds with their new solids can make weaning a more enjoyable experience for both you and your child.

3. Don't reduce your baby's breast/formula milk volume too quickly because milk feeds are still an important source of nutrition for your baby during their first year of life and beyond.

There are various misconceptions surrounding the whole issue of feeding your babies. One of them is not to let your baby get messy. Au contraire, let them get messy. Kids are at their best when they are having fun, and if your kid has to get a little dirty to get accustomed to solid foods, and then let him be.

Allow babies to get some food around their mouths; avoid wiping their mouth, hands, and face clean after each mouthful, e.g., with a spoon or a wet wipe. Also, don't be concerned if your child makes a face or spits food out. Remember that it can take 15 - 20 tries for your child to like something – so don't give up if they make a face when you give them broccoli!

Weaning is not new to only the infant; it is also new to the parents. Therefore, there are some important key points to note as you go ahead in the process. They include

- A baby needs small amounts of food at first.

- Slowly increase the amount of food a baby is given, ensuring that the intake matches the baby's growing appetite.

- Feed often and according to the baby's ability to chew and digest.

- Prepare nutritious mixes using foods of good quality. These protect babies from illness and help them gain weight in proportion to age.

- Feed foods that are high in energy and concentrated in nutrients.

- Please make sure all foods and the utensils used to prepare them are clean.

- Breast-feed for as long as possible.

- Give the baby care and attention to stimulate mental as well as physical growth.

- Feed more frequently during and after an illness. Give more liquids, especially if the baby has diarrhea.

- Whether you decide to go with traditional weaning or baby-led weaning, make sure it is the best choice for you and your baby.

- Be realistic with your expectations. Babies will take some time to learn something new, so don't rush the process and let them go at their own pace.

I mentioned earlier that weaning could be a challenging process, and you do not want to risk the possibility of introducing diseases to your baby. However, it is at this time that their immune system begins to develop as they start to encounter germs in their environment.

Because of this change, babies are more likely to contract infectious diseases starting around the age of 4-5 months, especially if they are not breastfed. As a result, any food prepared for babies should be stored and fed in very sanitary conditions.

Increasing the quantity and quality of the baby's food can be a very effective way to ensure that they are in good health. A weaning child has a small stomach but requires a lot of food for growth and activity. There are two main ways to ensure that these children receive adequate nutrition:

1. Excessive feeding – it might have crossed your mind, but no, I don't mean overfeeding your child. That will defeat the whole process. It means constant feeding at regular intervals.

2. Consuming foods with high nutrient content.

A family may consume up to three meals per day, with snacks in between. When they are awake, children of weaning age require something to eat every two hours. That's a lot, but that's what the whole process is all about.

NOTE: The smaller the child, the more frequently they need to be fed.

The food the family consumes is frequently filling and bulky. A child of weaning age requires food that is:

1. High in energy.

2. sustaining and,

3. Easily swallowed because it is soft.

These children require food combinations that have been specially prepared for them. Food does not have to be prohibitively expensive. You can usually make these meals from family foods, but they must be prepared in unique ways.

Lowering the risk of infection caused by the baby's food

Good, well-prepared food will keep a baby healthy and help him grow. Food tainted with germs will make the baby ill, afflicted with diarrhea, or other illnesses. Food can be contaminated with germs:

1. Before bringing it into the house,

2. while in storage

3. while preparing; or

4. After it's been prepared but before it's given to the baby

Breast milk is completely safe for infants. However, as soon as a baby is fed other foods, they are more likely to become infected with germs. This is why so many babies develop diarrhea while weaning.

To reduce the risk of an infection in a baby, parents should learn how to prepare weaning mixes carefully and under the most sanitary conditions possible. The utensils used to feed the baby should be kept clean, and ensure you wash your hands before preparing food and feeding the baby. Do not allow flies or other insects to land on your food.

Chapter 3

Key Steps in Baby Weaning

Baby weaning is a slow and steady process, and there are few key steps to take note of as you begin the process. It is not just about introducing your baby to new foods but also about the execution because that is, largely, what determines the success of the entire thing.

The first thing to note is the portions of food you serve.

The early tastes of solid foods (the first week) are more for educating your child about this new experience. Offer small, baby-sized servings of 1-2 teaspoons at each feed, gradually increasing to 2-4 tablespoons after the milk feed. Begin by offering your baby cereal once a day. Introduce a single ingredient food in small amounts at a time.

You can then link any allergies or intolerances to a specific food, such as starting with 1-2 teaspoons of baby cereal at one meal and gradually increasing the amount to 3-4 tablespoons once or twice a day.

The second thing is introducing one food at a time.

The predisposition to develop allergies is inherited. In most cases, an allergy will not be noticeable on the first occasion that the baby is exposed to the allergen.

It is always best to introduce one new food at a time for 3-5 days. This allows you to detect any negative reactions right away. Remove allergenic foods from the baby's diet and consult a healthcare professional to ensure the baby's diet remains nutritionally adequate. This systematic approach usually requires a minimum of 4–6 weeks between starting new food groups.

Repeatedly introduce new foods

DON'T EVER FORCE-FEED SOLID FOODS TO YOUR BABY. I know why I put that in capital letters. According to studies, you may have to feed your baby up to eight times before they accept it, so keep trying. This will instil healthy eating habits in children from an early age.

Start spoon-feeding.

Babies frequently spit out their first semi-solid food quite violently – not because they don't want the food, but because the tongue movement used in sucking is the only motion they are familiar with. They will have to learn an entirely new feeding technique. If their first attempts fail, you will be splashed with food! You might be smeared with food a few times, but that is all part of the fun!

Try not to get angry or frustrated; instead, persevere and enjoy your child's learning journey. Children who are healthy and hungry will eat if they are given a calm environment in which to do so. This is the first and most important factor to consider. When you or your baby is tired, it is not a good idea to introduce solid foods - your child probably needs the rest more than the meal. Feed your baby in an area where you can easily clean up any spills, and keep a clean cloth on hand to wipe up any spills. Finally, wear clothes that are simple to clean. You don't want to give yourself more work by wearing something difficult to wash.

Using a Spoon for the First Time

Pick a good spoon with a small, smooth edge. Plastic or rubberized spoons may be easier to use. Place a tiny spoon against the baby's lips and allow them to suck the contents. they'll have enough to taste and, if they like it, they'll keep eating. If you place the food on the front of your baby's tongue, it will simply dribble out.

Do not overfill the spoon or place it too far back in your baby's mouth. This force her to swallow without the option of refusing the food, and she may gag or even choke. Do not force your baby to eat. Allow him to suck the food off the spoon. Stop feeding him if the taste causes him to cry or if his closed lips say, "enough." You'll know when he is saying this. It can be hilarious at times.

Chapter 4

Baby Feeding based on Time

We have seen how weaning can be broken down into three different stages. Still, it would also help to know the feeding regime of a baby in the first 12 months of life to have a firm understanding of what the baby needs at different stages of their growth and development.

The first six months

Babies only require breast milk (or suitable first infant formula). If you are concerned that your baby is hungry or waking up more frequently, speak with your health visitor or a breastfeeding counselor who can advise you on how to maximize your breast milk or look at the milk feeds you give.

Changes in a baby's sleeping patterns before six months of age do not indicate hunger or the need for solids but are a normal part of development. Evidence suggests that a baby's waking and sleeping patterns are unrelated to whether or not they are fed breast milk or infant formula, but rather to their unique development pattern. During the first year of life, it is normal for breastfeeding to continue at night.

Close to six months

At around six months, infants are likely to show signs of preparedness for the introduction of solid foods alongside breast milk (or first infant formula). Babies should be able to sit up and hold their heads steady, pick up food with their hands, move food to their mouth, and swallow food. Every child is different, and others may learn to handle food in the mouth more slowly than others do, but you can offer a variety of greasy foods and soft finger foods.

At six to seven months

This stage is mostly about introducing new textures and tastes, building trust in your baby and the foods they can handle, and gradually increasing the number of solids you offer along with breast milk or first baby formula. As soon as you start introducing solids, you can include the baby in mealtimes with others, and babies will learn by watching others eat and mimicking their behavior. At mealtimes, you can include a small cup of water. Encourage your baby to participate in eating from the beginning. Be prepared for a messy situation!

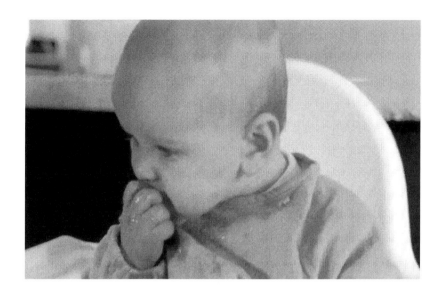

At seven to nine months

At this stage, babies will be able to eat three meals per day in addition to breast milk or first infant formula. Meals can be pulped or with soft lumps, and babies will enjoy having finger foods with meals, holding a spoon even if they are unable to feed themselves, and being included in mealtimes with other people. It can help them learn and have a little fun while doing it.

At this point, your baby will learn to do the following

1. Sit without support

2. Eat with a spoon, and

3. Start drinking from a cup.

Because he can chew, feed him chopped up and mashed food with small, soft lumps. Mash the food that the rest of the family is going to eat. During this stage, your baby will learn to chew more effectively.

Encourage him to eat by himself, but always be there to keep watch. Eventually, he will want to use his little fingers to explore food textures, shapes, and colors and to discover new food sensations. Introduce soft foods such as cooked vegetables like carrots, chopped soft fruit like pear and banana, and finger foods like toast.

Mashed or chopped foods are appropriate for "gumming," but when the front teeth (incisors) appear, babies are pretty much ready for soft finger foods. Start giving them cooked fruits and vegetables cut into small slices, as well as pasta that is small enough for their cute tiny hands to pick up.

Introduce one variety of finely ground meat (poultry, for example) and meat substitutes (dry beans, peas, and lentils) at a time, waiting about a week between each new food.

At ten to twelve months

Here, babies will be eating meals with larger soft lumps, handling a wider variety of finger foods, and becoming more skilful in their ability to pick up tiny bits of food and move them to their mouths. Also, they will be more confident in their use of a cup.

As your child's chewing and swallowing abilities improve, she will be ready to try more challenging, richer tastes and textures. When your baby reaches this age, she will be able to

1. Sit alone easily.

2. Feed herself using her hands and drinking from a cup with a lid.

3. Have one or two teeth and starts chewing

At this point, you can chop rather than mash your child's food. Also, encourage your baby to eat on her own. Your baby will now begin to follow the family meal routine.

After 12 months

At this point, your child is prepared to make the big transition from infancy to childhood. Also, your baby is already used to eating solid foods in addition to breastfeeding. Although breast milk or baby formula will provide fewer nutrients and energy than the food your baby eats by the age of one year, babies will progress to three meals and two nutritious sweet treats per day in the second year.

Breast milk provides babies with energy, nutrients, and protection from infection for as long as they are breastfed. Babies should be eating a variety of foods at meals, demonstrating increasing independence in eating, and drinking from a cup other than breast milk.

The first six months

Breast milk meets all of an infant's nutritional needs during the first six months of life and protects both the mother's and the baby's health. Breast milk is incredibly suited to the needs of a baby.

Its nutrient composition and the numerous bioactive factors it contains have enabled human populations to survive and develop for many generations. This is evident in colostrum, which is the first milk produced by the mother a few days after giving birth. It contains high concentrations of nutrients and antibodies, but it is in limited supply.

Breast milk cannot be substituted because its composition is dynamic – that is, it is a complete living substance that changes composition during feeds, as babies grow, and develop. It is unique to each mother and her baby and the environment in which they live. Human milk contains hundreds of bioactive molecules that cannot be replicated. The majority of these protect babies from infectious diseases and aid in the development of a strong, healthy immune system in the future.

Breast milk provides all of the fluid, energy, and nutrients that a baby requires and many important elements unique to human milk, such as immunoglobulins and anti-infective agents, which protect the infant from infections.

1. lactoferrin – a protein that aids in nutrient absorption and has antibacterial properties.

2. Special fatty acids that promote growth and development, as well as

3. Anti-viral, anti-bacterial, and living white blood cells that provide disease protection.

Breast milk is a baby's natural food, and it offers complete and comprehensive nutrition. Breast milk composition changes to meet the diverse needs of babies, whether during the day or over time. It has the distinctive ability to respond to an infant's immediate environment, providing a specific immune response from microorganisms and pathogens, which is aided by mothers and babies remaining in close contact with one another during breastfeeds.

Breastfeeding, according to women, can help build a strong bond between a mother and her baby, and many people get a lot of satisfaction from seeing their baby grow and develop and knowing that they were personally responsible for it.

Breastfeeding as a system of feeding has a lot of advantages for babies and mothers. Though we've mentioned some before, let's take a closer look at them in relation to the various participants.

Breastfeeding has a lot of advantages for babies. They include

1. Breastfed babies are less likely to develop gastrointestinal infections that cause diarrhea and, in some cases, dehydration. This is one of the most common reasons for a baby to visit the hospital during their first year of life.

2. Long-term conditions like weight gain, gluten sensitivity, cardiovascular disease, and type-one diabetes are less common in breastfed babies.

3. Many other conditions, such as sudden infant death syndrome (SIDS), allergic diseases such as respiratory problems and eczema, leukemia, and constipation, are less common in breastfed babies.

4. Other infections, such as respiratory illnesses, ear infections, and urinary tract infections, are rare in breastfed babies.

Breastfeeding is also good for a mother's health for the following reasons:

1. Breastfeeding mothers are less likely to develop breast cancer, ovarian cancer, and hip fractures.

2. Breastfeeding mothers have higher bone mineral density later in life.

3. Mums whom exclusively breastfeed for 3-4 months or longer are more likely to regain their pre-pregnancy weight.

Lastly, everyone benefits from this. Look at it from this angle. When a woman chooses to breastfeed, she benefits her family financially as well as the environment.

1. The dairy industry, which provides the cows' milk protein and lactose used in several baby formulas, is a major contributor to global greenhouse gas emissions and climate change.

2. Making infant formula in factories necessitates the use of a significant amount of natural resources and energy. Transporting infant formula to retail outlets requires the use of energy as well.

3. Breast milk does not require packaging.

4. Breastfeeding does not necessitate the use of bottles or teats.

5. There is no need for heat energy to compensate for breast milk or for feeding equipment to be washed.

6. Breast milk is completely waste-free.

When should you start mixing feed?

When a baby is about 4-6 months old, their mouth begins to develop the ability to accept non-liquid foods. Teeth begin to emerge, and the tongue no longer pushes solid food out of the mouth automatically. The stomach also begins to digest starch more efficiently. Babies can use their hands to put things into their mouths by the age of 9 months. Children are getting ready to eat solid foods at this age.

Babies who start eating semi-solid or solid foods before the age of 4-6 months consume less breast milk because their small stomachs are easily filled. As a result, they may not grow well. This will be reflected in the growth chart. Because of hunger and malnutrition, a child may begin to cry more frequently than usual.

On the other hand, children grow too big to thrive on breast milk alone after 4-6 months of age. For this reason, great care must be taken in deciding what foods to feed babies, and when and how to feed them. Every baby is unique. Larger babies may need to begin a mixed diet sooner than smaller babies do.

Breast milk alone is generally sufficient until the baby is at least four months old or weighing approximately 6-7 kg. Other foods are unnecessary and potentially harmful before this time. However, if other foods are not given in addition to breast milk by the age of six months, most babies will not get enough food to grow properly.

Keep in mind that a child is a member of the family. Babies are weaned by gradually introducing foods that the rest of the family consumes. Remember that these foods do not, at this time, replace breast milk; instead, they supplement the diet of breast milk. They cater to the baby's growing needs and aid in the developing the baby's ability to eat new foods.

Breast milk will continue to be a baby's primary source of nutrition for some time. It should be administered for as long as possible. Family foods will not completely replace breast milk until much later.

When Should Solid Foods be Introduced?

The goal of weaning is to introduce the baby to fresh tastes and textures as well as to teach them how to eat with a spoon. However, as with most things, it is best to start small! Baby cereals with a very smooth consistency are best for the first stage of weaning. Textured and lumpier foods and new flavor varieties should be introduced later in the weaning process to encourage chewing.

You can also introduce your baby to a wide range of baby cereals and flavors by adding vegetables, honey, fruits, or even meat and fish. The more variety there is, the better! One major thing to be aware of is the exact time you decide to wean your baby. You don't want to risk getting to it too early or late, as this can have adverse effects.

Introducing weaning too soon;

1. Obstructs breastfeeding (reduces sucking intensity).

2. May cause allergies and food intolerance.

3. Could lead to a higher risk of overfeeding and infectious diarrhea.

Introducing weaning too late:

1. It is possible that this will result in malnutrition and a delay in growth.

In the midst of all these, do not forget your role as a parent and what you're expected to do.

1. As adults, you are in charge of what and when your children eat.

2. The parent has control over the types of food served at meals and snacks.

3. It is up to the children to decide how much they eat.

Their appetites and how much they eat vary from day to day. As such, children should never be forced to eat.

There are different ways baby foods can be categorized; one is to classify them according to the nature of the food given. This will include;

The first foods

Your baby's first foods can include puréed or soft cooked fruits and vegetables such as apples, pears, potatoes, carrots, or sweet potatoes, all of which should be cooled before eating.

Finger foods

Food that has been cut into pieces large enough for your baby to hold in their tiny fists with a portion sticking out is known as finger food. Pieces that are the size of your finger are ideal. This is how your baby learns to chew. Try holding bite-size pieces of soft, ripe banana or avocado.

Next foods

Once your baby has become accustomed to the foods listed above, they can eat soft-cooked meats such as chicken, mashed fish (check for any bones), pasta, noodles, toast, pieces of roti, beans, rice, and mashed hard-boiled eggs. In addition, select products with no extra sugar or salt or less sugar and salt, and there should be no sugar or salt added.

Fluids

From around six months, give fluids such as water, Rooibos tea, or small amounts of fresh fruit juice with meals.

Emotional and mental growth in weaning

Weaning is a period of significant behavioral change for both the baby and the parents. Babies are becoming more curious about the world around them and more self-sufficient in their actions. Mothers initially devote almost all of their time to their newborn children. This change during weaning.

Mothers must return to their regular work schedules or pursue new responsibilities and interests. As a result, the close bonds between mothers and their babies must gradually loosen during weaning. Babies will be separated from their mothers for lengthy periods. Mothers may need to rely on family members to care for their babies as they return to their regular duties inside or outside the home.

Changes in the way kids are cared for during the weaning period can result in babies not being fed properly or becoming upset and unhappy. Babies, for example, may lose their appetites while their mothers are away. If the person caring for them is careless or unsure what to do, they may be given too little food. These dangers can usually be avoided if you are aware of them.

Correct feeding is not the only factor that contributes to healthy growth and development. When babies are sick, they require emotional stimulation as well as the proper type of care. All of these factors must be considered for successful weaning.

Chapter 5

Weaning Foods

We have come to the critical parts of the discourse. This is where you as a parent must pay close attention so you don't make any errors. Let's take a close look at weaning foods on the basis of the three weaning stages mentioned above.

Stage 1

At this stage, begin with 1 teaspoon of soft, smooth puréed food. You can use up to 6 teaspoons at a time. Then, at another mealtime, introduce solid food. Increase gradually to 2-3 meals per day, with 5-10 teaspoons at each. I'll strongly advise you to start with thin purées that will thicken as the baby becomes accustomed to solid food. This will allow the baby to learn the following.

1. Eating food with a spoon.

2. Moving food from the front to the back of the mouth in preparation for swallowing.

3. Working with thicker purées.

Examples of the foods, which could be given at this stage, include purée made from meat, poultry, and fish. Cereals such as baby rice. Pureed vegetables like carrot, parsnip, turnip, broccoli, cauliflower, butternut squash, and courgette. Fruit purées of bananas, apples, pears, peaches, apricots, plums, and melon. Suitable drinks include breast milk, infant formula and cooled boiled water.

Stage 2

This stage is characterized by giving three meals per day, each containing about 2 to 4 tablespoons of food. In between main meals, have two to three snacks, including finger foods. Food should be served prior to milk feeding. Also, give the baby some beverages poured from a cup or beaker. The food textures at this stage should include;

1. Thicker pureés are made by adding less liquid to the purée.

2. Finger food that is soft

3. Mash the food with a little liquid and serve.

4. Mix textures by incorporating mashed or grated food into baby's regular purées.

As the babies transition from thick purées to mashed foods, and then to foods with soft lumps, they will learn to start feeding themselves soft finger foods, and taking a drink from a beaker or cup.

Foods, which can be given here, are similar to those in Stage 1, but now includes meat, poultry, and fish, well-cooked eggs, cereals for breakfast, bread, rice, and pasta. You could also add cheese (pasteurized), yogurt, and pasteurized cow's milk can be used to moisten foods in small amounts. Suitable drinks include breast milk on demand, infant formula and cooled boiled water.

Finger foods

Finger foods are small pieces of food that babies can grasp and feed themselves. Babies frequently demonstrate their readiness to begin eating complementary foods by showing an interest in holding foods and putting foods to their mouth, and it is critical to encourage eating independence.

After 6 months, babies can pick things up with their entire hand, and the perfect finger foods to provide are those that are soft and easy to bite and chew. It's a good idea to make finger foods slightly larger than a baby's hand so they can grip things in their fist. A good guideline is the size of an adult finger.

Slices of omelette, homemade pancakes, toast, bread, pita bread, or chapati, peeled apple, banana, raw or cooked green beans, cooked carrot sticks, or cheese sticks are all appropriate finger foods. Ignore biscuits and rusks so that your baby does not develop the expectation of sweet snacks. Sugar is present in even low-sugar rusks.

This may appear to be progressing quickly, but you'll be surprised at how quickly your baby can advance - one of the advantages of waiting until 6 months to begin weaning. As an expert in early child development, I've had the opportunity to speak with a lot of moms all over the world, and many a time, most of them are concerned about their babies choking on lumps, but a baby is more likely to choke on liquid than food, so there's no need to worry as long as you always supervise your baby eating.

If you postpone giving 'lumpy' or finger foods, your baby may refuse to eat 'lumpy' foods as they grow older.

The Do's and Don'ts of feeding finger foods

Like most things involving children, there is a right way to do it.

1. Check for pips, stones, hard skin, or stringy bits in finger foods.

2. Begin with soft or cooked vegetables and fruit.

3. Avoid whole grapes, apple or carrot chunks, nuts, and popcorn because these are the foods that babies are most likely to choke on.

4. Avoid small, hard foods as well as those in gelatinous pieces. Keep an eye on your baby while he or she is eating.

5. If you're serving raw food, make sure it's thoroughly washed.

6. Don't ever leave babies unattended while they are trying to eat. Try to pay special attention when they are eating finger foods to encourage them, and to ensure that they do not choke on any bits that break off in their mouth as they develop their eating skills.

Stage 3

At this stage, begin to target three meals of 4-6 tablespoons each. Also, give two to three small snacks and babies should be able to handle more than two textures in a single meal. All drinks (except breastfeeds) are consumed from a cup or beaker. The food textures preferred here include foods that are lumpy, chopped foods, and tougher finger foods. As a result of that, a wide range of foods and textures are available.

All these will help the child to start self-feeding. In addition, chunkier textures will aid in speech and chewing, as well as increase the variety of the baby's diet in later childhood. At this point, most homemade family foods (without adding salt, gravies, sauces, sauce packets or jars, or sugar) are now acceptable. Like in the first two stages, the drinks that can be given to the babies include breast milk on demand, infant formula and cooled boiled water.

Classes of Weaning Foods

Staple food

A soft, thick, creamy porridge made from the community's major staple is an excellent first food to give a baby, along with breast milk. Every society has a favorite food. When asked about their diet, it is frequently the first food that comes to mind. The staple food contains starch and is consumed by the majority of the community at every meal.

It is usually cheaper than other types of food. The staple differs from one country to the next. Rice, wheat maize, cassava yam, potato, or something else could be used. Families in rural areas will most likely spend a significant amount of time growing, storing, and cooking the staple food.

The staple is an excellent base for preparing babies' first weaning foods because it is typically less expensive than other types of food, is readily available, and provides the majority of the carbohydrates (starch) and other nutrients required for growth.

Examples of staples – for the purpose of this topic, let's categorize staples into three classes.

1. Cereals - examples include rice, maize, wheat, oats, barley, sorghum, millet, etc.

2. Roots and underground vegetables- examples are Yam, cocoyam, taro, cassava, potato, and sweet potato.

3. Starchy fruits, which include bananas, plantains, breadfruit, etc.

Staple foods are a good starting point for infant foods, but they are insufficient. Other foods are also required. This other food is originally breast milk. However, as the baby grows older, different types of food are required. These other food types are:

1. Peas and beans

2. Food from animals

3. Green leafy vegetables and orange vegetables

4. Fats and oils

5. fruits

Peas & Beans

These are healthy foods. When combined with cereal staples, they are just as nutritious as animal foods and are frequently less expensive. Pea and bean skins are harder to digest, but careful preparation overcomes this issue. Soak them first, and then cook them until tender. The skins are then broken up or removed by sieving. Peas and beans are also beneficial to the elderly members of the family.

To ensure that babies like the taste, mix small amounts of peas and beans with the staple porridge at first. The amount can then be gradually increased. Nuts and seeds are also nutritious additions to the traditional porridge.

There are numerous varieties of peas and beans in the world. Chickpeas, cowpeas, peanuts (groundnuts), pigeon peas, lentils, split peas, blackeyed beans, red beans, navy beans, broad beans, french beans, soya beans, sesame seeds, melon seeds, mung beans, and lima beans are just a few examples.

Dark green leafy vegetables and orange vegetables

Vegetables are excellent first foods to introduce to infants. To begin, try veggies one at a time to introduce new flavors, and then experiment with combos. Add potatoes or sweet potatoes to thicken smooth or mashed vegetables.

Make sure that a broad range of vegetable foods is available and that foods from all of the vegetable colors are introduced into babies' diets. Infants will be drawn to brightly colored foods, but there is no need to use pricey vegetables. Using vegetables in season and from local sources will save you the most money.

Many different green leafy vegetables are grown in various locations around the world. In general, the darker the color of the leaves, the higher the nutritional value. Cooking causes leafy vegetables to soften and shrink.

They can then be individually chopped and mixed into a child's favorite porridge. They are also very beneficial to children. There are numerous methods for making them soft enough to eat. They can then be eaten on their own or mixed into a child's regular diet. Examples include Spinach, kale, amaranth, parsnips, pumpkin leaves, avocado, butternut squash, broccoli, carrot, sweet cassava leaves, green beans, mushroom etc.

Food from animals

These protein-rich foods are also high in other essential nutrients. Infants can be given a wide range of protein foods, including meat, fish, eggs. Many of these foods are high in iron and zinc, both of which are essential nutrients for infants.

Almost all animal foods are nutritious. However, they are frequently expensive. They are available in a variety of forms, including

1. Meat, fish, and organ meats such as liver.

2. Milk from various animals, including milk-based foods such as cheese and yoghurt. Although butter is derived from animals, it is not included in this category. It is categorized as fat.

3. Egg.

To make it easier for babies to eat, meat is frequently finely chopped or pounded with a pestle. Fish bones that could choke the baby must be removed with extreme caution. Animal food can be mixed with the staple and fed to babies.

Fats & Oils

Oils and fats provide valuable energy for young children. They also soften and make food easier to swallow. Sugar and honey can also provide extra energy, but not as effectively as oils and fats.

Examples of fats and oils

Corn oil, palm oil, sunflower oil, groundnut (peanut) oil, coconut oil, and coconut milk are all oils (that is the milk from the flesh of the coconut, not the coconut water). Examples of fat are ghee, butter, margarine, and lard.

Fruits

Fruit can be introduced once babies have accepted other savory tastes. Fruit, which has a natural sweetness, will be accepted quite easily and quickly by most babies, as opposed to vegetables. Fruits are safe for young children if they are thoroughly cleaned. Start handing fruits to babies after they have learned to eat their staple foods.

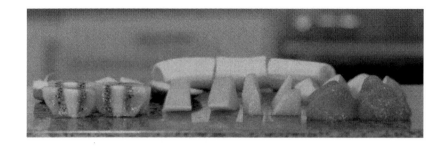

The fruits can either be mashed or juiced. Cook or mash soft fruits to soften them, and if you're going to make a smooth version, make sure the fruit is free of pips and skin. Make certain that the fruits are clean so that no infectious diseases are introduced. If you want to dilute fruit purees or juices with water, ensure that the water is very clean. When serving fruit as finger foods, keep the pieces soft and manageable, and avoid chunks of apple or harder fruits.

An ideal food mixture for a young child contains all the following types of food.

1. The staple.

2. Peas and beans.

3. Animal-derived foods.

4. Dark green leafy vegetables and orange vegetables.

5. Fruits.

6. Fats and oils

7. Breast milk.

A baby does not have to eat everything at once. If the family does not have access to animal food on a daily basis, peas and beans are a good substitute.

Fussy eaters

As your baby grows into a toddler, he or she will have specific food preferences. Not all children are picky when it comes to food, but for some, this is the moment at which they gain independence. Babies who exclusively eat their favorites are unlikely to develop a taste for other meals and may develop fussiness. It may take up to eight attempts for your infant to enjoy new flavors.

Here are some other ways you could try to urge your child to eat in order to encourage them to try new foods:

1. Make feeding more enjoyable by offering food in various forms on their plates.

2. Make "yummy" noises to let them know the food is excellent.

3. Serve them little portions of various foods and keep track of which ones they prefer.

4. If your baby rejects new foods, try again and be gentle with them.

What foods should be combined for weaning?

First, babies will consume a small amount of porridge made from the local staple, boiled in water or milk, and nourished with a small amount of oil or fat. Porridge should be thick or semi-solid rather than thin and runny. Porridge that is overly watery does not provide enough nutrients for newborns.

It takes a few days for the baby to develop a taste for the new flavor, so he or she may only eat a small amount at first. This is not a problem because one to two teaspoonful is sufficient. Breast milk will provide the majority of the baby's nutrition. Later on, the infant will be able to eat more solid food and love the taste.

Most babies will be eating and enjoying the staple cereal in less than two weeks. The diet can then be supplemented with other items. They should be chopped finely or diced and served separately or with the cereal. Peas and beans, as well as animal food, are essential and should be provided to the baby with the porridge when available. Oil or fat should be used at all times. Other food types can be offered less often.

Roots, comparable underground vegetables, or starchy fruits are less nutritious than grains. If you are using them for porridge, it is critical to add animal items, such as meat, fish, eggs, or milk, as soon as the baby is acclimated to the porridge, which should be within a week.

2. Two mixes

A two-mix is a staple that has another class of food added to it. Two-mixes are very nutritious and are used as the major component of many meals. They can be expressed in three ways.

- Staple + peas or beans

- Staple + food from animals

- Staple + dark green leafy vegetables or orange vegetables

3. Three mixes

Three-mixes are superior to two-mixes. They consist of the staple as well as two other food kinds. There are three kinds of nutrient-dense three-mixes.

- Staple + peas or beans + food from animals

- Staple + peas or beans + dark green leafy vegetables or orange vegetables

- Staple + food from + dark green leafy vegetables animals or orange vegetables

4. Four mixes

Four-mixes are the best of the bunch. These include all four major food groups. They are a combination of the staples, peas or beans, animal food, and dark green leafy vegetables or orange vegetables. A good example is:

- Staple + peas or beans + food from animals + dark green leafy vegetables or orange vegetables

Chapter 6

Food Preparation

Once your infant begins eating solid foods, you will need to prepare them. It is also beneficial to the baby's immune system because their stomachs are more susceptible to illnesses. The following are key points to take note of during food preparation.

1. Before preparing any meal for your infant, thoroughly wash your hands.

2. Boiling water should be used for cooking and cleaning utensils.

3. Store your baby's cutlery on a different shelf and rinse them with boiling water before serving.

4. If the food is frozen, defrost it completely before cooking it, unless the food label specifies otherwise.

5. Never refreeze previously frozen food.

6. Baby food that has been made ahead of time should be cooled rapidly and then refrigerated.

Safety precautions for some specific foods

1. **Fruit with skins or seeds:** Remove the seeds and peel the fruit before giving it to your child. Fruits can be diced, cooked, and mashed as well.

2. **Fish or chicken with bones:** Carefully separate the meat from the bones and then cut it into small pieces. Examine the meat carefully for any traces of bones.

3. **Peanut butter:** If your child is of an age where they can safely take peanut butter, you should be aware that a teaspoon of peanut butter could obstruct the windpipe. Peanut butter can also adhere to the lining of the throat

and windpipe, preventing a youngster from breathing. If you must give your child peanut butter, use only a little on a slice of bread or a cracker.

4. **Hot dogs and sausages:** Cut these meats into thin pieces. Before you cut them, you may want to remove the skin.

5. **Grapes:** Before serving, peel and crush the grapes.

6. Always mash beans (particularly large beans) before serving.

7. **Peas:** Although peas are small in themselves, a youngster who consumes more than one pea at a time may choke.

8. **Whole carrots:** A baby may choke if he or she takes a large enough bite. Carrots can be cooked and sliced into smaller bits, or raw carrots can be cut into thin slices.

9. Finally, and most importantly, keep the baby upright in his high chair while eating, and never leave a baby alone with food.

Foods to Avoid Giving Your Baby

Now that we have looked at the different kinds of foods you can give to your baby, let us take a little time to see those foods which are not recommended and why.

1. Salt

Because babies' kidneys are not properly developed, no salt should be added to their foods. Leave out the salt when cooking for the family, or remove a small portion for them and cook it separately so your baby can share family meals. You should also avoid foods high in salt, such as packet soups, stock cubes, crisps, bacon, and smoked meats.

2. Sugar

Do not add sugar to your baby's food or drinks. Sugar may encourage a sweet tooth and lead to tooth decay when the first teeth appear.

3. Honey

Please, honey should not be given to a child before the age of one year, even if it is used to relieve coughs, and I know why I said please. Honey may contain a type of bacteria that can produce toxins in the baby's intestines and cause a potentially fatal illness (infant botulism). After the age of one, the baby's intestine matures and bacteria cannot grow, but keep in mind that honey is also a sugar and can cause the same issues, such as tooth decay.

4. Nuts

Because of the risk of choking, whole nuts of any kind are not recommended for children under the age of five. For the most part, products containing nuts, such as peanut butter, are safe for children. Before giving nuts to your baby for the first time, consult your GP, health professional, or medical allergy expert if there is a family history of conditions such as asthma, eczema, or hay fever (ie parents, brothers, or sisters).

Protecting your baby's teeth

The development of teeth can be one of the most challenging stages in a baby's life. It usually comes with episodes of crying, lack of sleep, and lack of appetite, which can prove very difficult for the parents, especially when they are not equipped with the right knowledge to deal with the problem. In that light, it is very important to start caring for your baby's tooth as soon as they appear and begin to eat solid foods. The following steps should give you a head start.

- Avoid offering sugary foods or drinks.

- Never serve anything other than milk or water in a bottle. Start at six months by introducing a cup.

- Never dip dummies in anything sweet or use sweet foods to appease children.

- Start brushing your baby's teeth twice a day, every day, as soon as they appear. Apply a small amount of fluoridated toothpaste to your teeth.

- The most tooth-friendly drinks are milk and water (boiled and cooled for children under one year of age).

- Give sugar-free medications.

- Choose healthy snacks, such as fresh fruit (not dried), vegetables, plain yogurt, cheese, and bread, as you introduce your baby to family foods.

- Do not give fruit juices

- Prepare homemade meals

- When foods are packaged and labeled as 'no added sugar' or 'low sugar', it does not entirely imply sugar free. So be careful when dealing with such kinds of products

- Only give healthy sugary treats such as dried fruit at mealtimes

- Don't ever add sugar to their foods,

- Do not allow your baby to suck from pouches of fruit puree or smoothies.

- Begin cleaning gently with a soft toothbrush and water when their first tooth appears.

- You might want to start brushing your baby's teeth as soon as they appear (last thing at night and then once again). However, children under the age of two should not be using fluoride toothpaste. A very small amount of toothpaste can be used after 2 years.

Lastly, food products high in fat, sugar, or salt, such as biscuits, crisps, chocolate, sweets, ice cream, or fizzy drinks, should not be included in your kid's regular diet at any age. Register your baby with a dentist as soon as the first tooth appears (around

6 months of age) and continue to take them for dental exams as often as your dentist recommends.

How to Serve Drinks

Babies should be introduced to drinking from a cup or beaker at the age of 6 months, and they should be deterred from drinking from a bottle at the age of 12 months. For this part, the best option is to use open-topped cups or ones with a free-running spout to avoid having to 'suck.' Sucking drinks from a bottle teat or spout increases the amount of time the drink is in contact with the teeth, which can lead to dental issues.

 Baby cups are useful for introducing drinking from a cup because they are easy to hold and have a small volume of liquid. Water should be boiled and cooled before being given to children under the age of six months, but tap water is safe for all infants over the age of six months. Other than milk and water, there is no need for drinks during the first year. Baby juices or herbal drinks are unnecessary, and because they contain sugar, they can harm a baby's teeth.

Drinks that should not be consumed

1. Soft drinks, squashes, fruit juices, and cordials, with or without sugar

2. Drinks containing caffeine or stimulants

3. Drinks with artificial sweeteners

4. Rice milk or rice beverages

5. Any kind of tea or coffee

6. Alcohol

Still on the topic of food, a few budding questions I am normally asked by mothers and parents generally include how much do I feed my kid? How do I know he is satisfied? How can I tell when he wants me to stop? All these will be discussed as we go on.

Let's dive right into them. How much food should you give your baby?

Countless moms bring this up, but actual figures are useless. Babies will eat in accordance with their growth rate. It is critical to understand your baby's behavior because it will indicate when she has had enough.

It is critical to understand when to begin and when to stop feeding. Your baby's behavior will indicate when she is content. When your baby is satisfied, he or she will exhibit the following behavior:

At stage 1 (first six months)

1. Nipple is released, and the head is withdrawn.

2. Uses hands to obstruct the mouth.

3. Increases awareness of one's surroundings.

4. Bites nipples. I know this can be very painful and annoying, but refrain from hitting your child whenever this happens. I promise you that you don't want to develop this habit, in the event that this happens, quickly pull away.

During stage 2 (seven to nine months)

1. Changes posture

2. Keep the mouth tightly shut.

3. Shakes his head, as if to say "no."

4. Enjoys playing with utensils

5. Increased activity of the hands.

6. tosses utensils

At stage three (ten to twelve months)

The behaviors here include all those from stage 2 with a few additions.

1. Mumbles with the tongue and the lips.

2. Returns a bottle or cup to the mother.

Stage 4 (twelve months and above)

1. Say "no" to the food.

2. Refuses to eat any further

3. Plays around with the food

4. Toss the food away.

Food Allergies

A food allergy is a harmful, frequently delayed reaction, to a food, beverage, food additive, or molecule found in foods that generates symptoms in one or more human organs and systems. Food hypersensitivity is used to refer widely to both food allergies and food intolerances.

A wide range of foods can induce allergic reactions, but cow's milk, soy, eggs, wheat, peanuts, tree nuts, fish, and shellfish account for 90% of all allergic reactions. Other food allergies may be deemed "rare" if they impact less than one person per 10,000 people. The use of hydrolyzed milk baby formula versus regular milk baby formula appears to have no effect on the risk.

When solids are introduced too early, before 4-6 months, there is a higher risk of allergies. The immune system of a baby may react to proteins included in diets other than breast milk. These reactions may cause allergic reactions in the newborn, such as eczema, diarrhea, or vomiting. When one or both parents have a family history of allergies, their child is more likely to acquire an allergy. Use the following as a guide when dealing with allergenic foods.

1. It is recommended to postpone the introduction of solids for as long as feasible.

2. When introducing solid foods, introduce one at a time during a 3-5 day period.

3. Before introducing allergic food items, consult with your healthcare practitioner first.

How to Deal with Choking

When your baby encounters a novel texture for the first time, he or she may gag out of surprise. If she does, saddle her over your forearm, with her head lower than her torso, and her weight supported by your thigh. Pat her on the back firmly with your heel and encourage her to cough until the food is released.

Talk soothingly to her and softly touch her back, and she'll be able to swallow more easily. Note that there's a possibility for your baby to lose consciousness, so learn how to provide first aid for choking so that never happens.

Weaning is a major learning experience for both you and your baby, and as long as you can provide safe foods, your baby's gums are perfectly capable of chewing soft, mashed foods. Babies, on the other hand, can gag a few times during their first few efforts at eating. This can be as a result of putting too much food in their mouths at once or because the food is pushed too far back.

In principle, this is indeed a positive thing since the gag reflex is a protective mechanism that keeps you from choking! It forces your infant to move food from the back of the throat to the front, preventing it from being lodged. As a result, your child will know what not to do the next time.

What's the difference between gagging and choking? A lot of people confuse these two terms, but they are not entirely the same. Gagging is basically a feeling of illness with a tendency to vomit, while coughing occurs when a foreign item (i.e. food, drinks) is stuck in a person's airway. As such;

1. A gagging kid appears to be coughing lightly and may make a small noise.

2. A choking baby will appear afraid, will be unable to breathe, and will make a noise.

Safety precautions to avoid choking

Preparing food for young children in ways that lessen their risk of choking is the greatest strategy to avoid choking. Avoid foods that can cause choking, such as:

*   Nuts

*   Pop corn

- Hamburgers

- Peanut butter chunks

- Raw vegetables,

- Raisins

- Whole grapes

- Meat or cheese chunks

- Apple chunks and other fruit portions

Chapter 7

Frequently Asked Questions

Parents normally have a lot of questions in relation to their baby's feeding and their general wellbeing. Because of the misconceptions that have developed over the years on these issues, I have decided to go over them in this chapter.

1. What should I do if my kid refuses to eat?

Do not be concerned because babies and young children, like adults, sometimes have "off days." If food is rejected, take it away and replace it with breast milk or formula milk. If the situation persists, call your local public health nurse.

2. My 12-week-old infant is not sleeping through the night. Is it possible that giving him solid meals now will help him sleep?

There is no evidence that giving a baby solid food affects how long he or she sleeps.

3. When my child was born, he was a huge baby. Isn't he going to require solid meals sooner?

Your baby's birth weight has no bearing on when they will be ready for solid food; their digestive tract and kidneys develop at the same level as other newborns. Solid food should be introduced as early as 17 weeks of age, ideally closer to 26 weeks of age. Remember to keep an eye out for developmental indicators that show whether or not your baby is ready to start eating solid meals.

4. When I feed my infant lumpier food, he gags. What should I do?

Gagging is a natural response that babies experience as they learn to eat and swallow. We all have a 'gag' reflex, which is a response that aids in the prevention of choking. Gagging indicates that your infant is guarding his or her airway and removing food from the back of his or her mouth.

Gagging forces food into your baby's mouth, allowing him or her to chew it more thoroughly or swallow a lesser amount. Try to remain calm. As your baby grows and learns to control the amount of food he or she swallows, they should gag less frequently.

If you have any questions or concerns regarding your baby's gagging, contact your Public Health Nurse or a doctor. Some parents may be inclined to avoid feeding lumpier textures, but in order for gagging to decrease, you must continually introduce lumpier textures to their baby so that they learn to chew and swallow.

5. Can I give my infant bottled water?

Bottled water is not sanitary and should be boiled and cooled in the same manner as tap water for all newborns until they reach the age of 12 months. It is advised to avoid using bottled water labeled 'Natural Mineral Water,' as it may include greater levels of salt and other minerals. However, if no other water is available, it can be used for as brief a time as possible because it is critical to keep your infant hydrated.

6. Is it necessary for my infant to consume additional formula milk?

If your child eats a good diet that includes iron-rich foods, there should be no need for additional formula milk. Continue to use breast milk or formula milk until the child is one year old. Breast milk or cow's milk should be the major drink from the age of one year.

7. Is microwaving infant food safe?

There is a risk of 'hotspots' and scorching your baby's mouth because the food is heated unevenly. As a result, while using microwaves to heat meals for newborns and small children, you must exercise extreme caution. If you want to heat food in a microwave, it must be properly heated, allowed to stand for a few moments, thoroughly mixed, and left to cool to feeding temperature.

8. My kid is refusing to eat. Is he picky about what he eats?

It is common for newborns and young kids to shun food on occasion. Remember that it may take up to 15 attempts before they accept a new dish. Make sure they aren't consuming too much milk, drinks, or snacks near mealtimes. Reduce distractions by turning off the television and eating family meals with your child so they may learn from you.

If they refuse particular foods, give it another try a few days later. Do not serve sweet items like yogurt instead of savory foods, as kids will quickly learn that if they decline dinner, they can still obtain dessert. Simply take the food and set it aside until the next meal or snack. For the most part, this is a passing phase.

Chapter 8

Bowel Movements

During the course of this journey, you will notice that your baby's bowel movements will change. This will include changes in color and texture, and for some parents, this can be a little scary and very confusing, especially when you don't know what those changes mean.

As your baby begins to eat new foods, their bowel movements will change, and their poop will thicken, darken, and smell more. Let's go over all the possible colors you might encounter.

1. Mustard yellow

If you are solely breastfeeding your baby and his or her stool is bright or mustard yellow (and occasionally slightly orangish), then big congrats, your kid's poop is normal.

2. Tan

If your infant is on formula and their stool is a yellowish-brown color and slightly solid (similar to a thin peanut sauce), then it is normal.

3. Lime green

This color of baby excrement usually indicates that there is some intestinal trouble. Lime green poop can also indicate a stomach virus. Stomach bug poop is typically frothy and/or mucousy. Another reason your breastfed baby's stool is green could be a reaction to anything you're eating. Finally, if the baby has lately had spinach or kale, it could provide an answer to the question "Why is the baby's poop green?"

Always contact your healthcare professional if you see any changes that cause you concern, as they will be able to rule out any potential issues.

4. Forest green

Dark green feces are a common occurrence in the stool of a newborn who is taking some nutrients. It could also be the change from meconium to normal feces. Consult your doctor about possible substances that could modify the color of your baby's stool.

5. Brown

As she begins to eat more solids, her feces will begin to turn brown. Don't be alarmed as this is perfectly normal.

6. White

A baby's stool that is chalky white or grey can indicate that his liver is not making enough bile. When you notice this, call your pediatrician right away. Another critical condition is when your baby's poop causes them pain, and this might mean that they may be constipated. Make sure to provide them with plenty of water, fruits, and veggies.

Printed in Great Britain
by Amazon

84392081R00054